Red Eyes or Blue Feathers

A Book About Animal Colors

by Patricia M. Stockland   illustrated by Todd Ouren

Special thanks to our advisers for their expertise:

Zoological Society of San Diego
San Diego Zoo
San Diego, California

Susan Kesselring, M.A., Literacy Educator
Rosemount-Apple Valley-Eagan (Minnesota) School District

PICTURE WINDOW BOOKS
Minneapolis, Minnesota

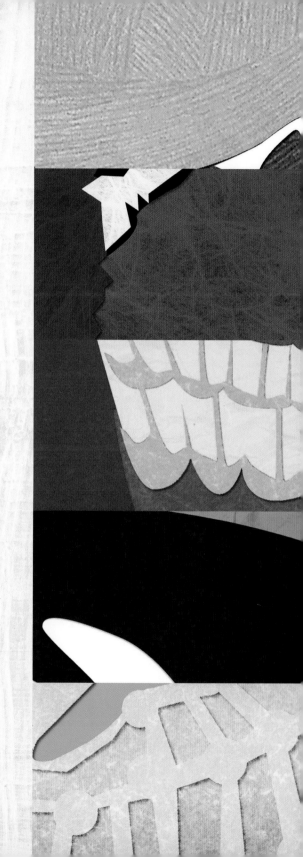

Managing Editor: Catherine Neitge
Creative Director: Terri Foley
Art Director: Keith Griffin
Editor: Christianne Jones
Designer: Todd Ouren
Page production: Picture Window Books
The illustrations in this book were prepared digitally.

Picture Window Books
5115 Excelsior Boulevard
Suite 232
Minneapolis, MN 55416
877-845-8392
www.picturewindowbooks.com

Printed in the United States of America.

Library of Congress Cataloging-in-Publication Data
Stockland, Patricia M.
Red eyes or blue feathers : a book about animal colors /
by Patricia M. Stockland ; illustrated by Todd Ouren.
p. cm. — (Animal wise)
Includes bibliographical references (p.   ) and index.
ISBN 1-4048-0931-7 (hardcover)
1. Animals—Color—Juvenile literature. I. Ouren, Todd, ill.
II. Title.

QL767.S77 2004
591.47'2—dc22
                                          2004020800

Color Adaptations

What's the best way to survive in the wild? Adaptation! Color is one way to adapt. So how does an animal's color help it survive?

Some animals have colors that help them hide from hungry predators. Other animals use their color to keep from being seen while they hunt. Colors even help animals find mates or talk to each other.

Read on to find out why some animals have such clever colors.

Red-eyed Treefrog

Bright, red eyes shine in the night. The red-eyed treefrog is wide awake.

During the day, this tiny frog hides its bright colors by closing its eyes and tucking up its legs. The red-eyed treefrog's shiny green back blends in with the trees. Predators think the little frog is a leaf.

The vertical pupils of the red-eyed treefrog help it see better at night. Daytime frogs usually have horizontal pupils.

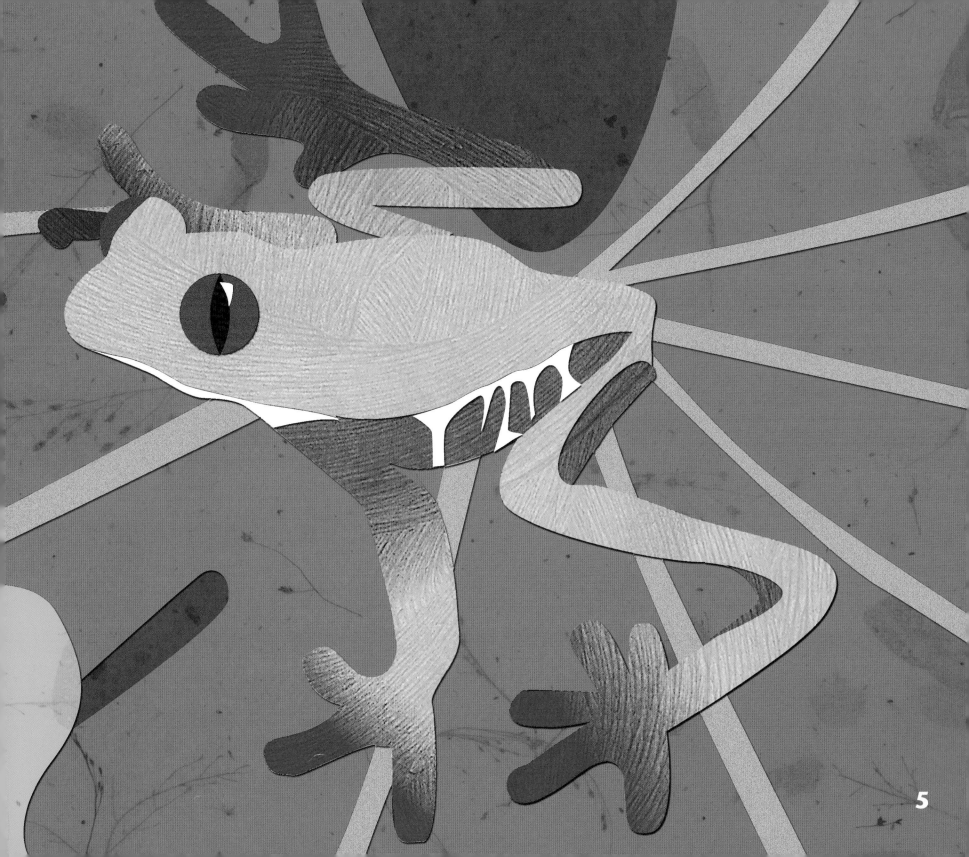

Polar Bear

White fur surrounds a shiny black nose. A polar bear slowly lumbers across the snow.

The polar bear's snow-colored coat blends in with the Arctic tundra. Its favorite treat is seal blubber. As the bear sits on the edge of the ice, a seal comes up for air. The seal doesn't see the giant paw grabbing for it. *Grrr!*

Polar bears are not actually white. Their fur is transparent, or clear. Light reflects off it and makes it appear white or yellowish.

Red Fox

Rusty-colored fur rustles through the woods. A red fox follows a scent.

This small fox finds food in many places. Its red coat and dark tail help it blend in with plants and trees. Neither predators nor prey can see the sly fox. Being able to hide so well helps this animal live and survive in many different places.

The red fox will eat almost anything, including insects, fruit, and leftover food from people's garbage cans.

Seahorse

Yellow, green, and brown seaweed swishes in the shallow sea. A small seahorse swishes in the seaweed, too.

The seahorse is a slow swimmer. Its yellow-brown armor helps it blend in with the seaweed. Larger fish can't see the seahorse hiding.

The seahorse can quickly change color to blend in better with its surroundings. It also changes color when it mates.

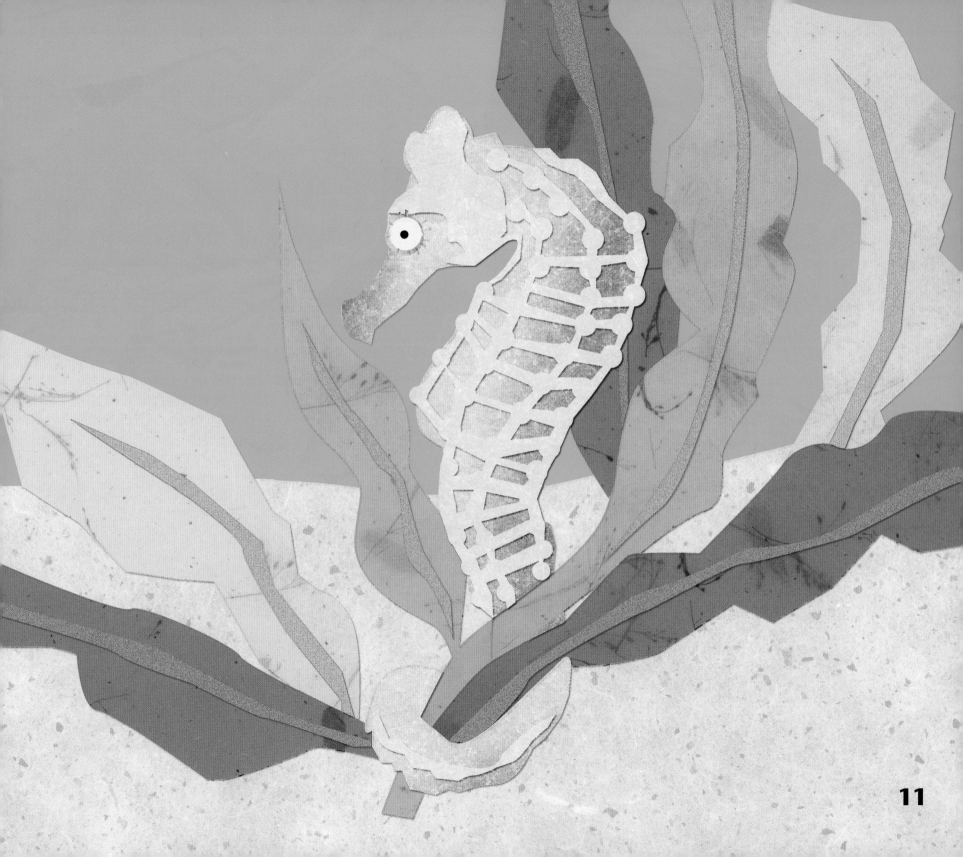

Killer Whale

A huge, black and white animal glides through the water. The killer whale is ready to attack.

This ocean mammal is a smart hunter. Black and white markings help this large animal hide. From below, its white belly looks like sunlight. From above, its black back becomes part of the ocean's shadows.

Killer whales use a lot of hunting tricks. Some swim under chunks of ice and tip them. Resting seals slide right into the water.

Macaw

Red, blue, yellow, and green feathers float in the air. A colorful macaw lands in the trees.

Macaws are some of the brightest birds around. The fancy colors fit well in their rain forest homes. These bold colors help the parrots blend into their surroundings.

The white skin around a macaw's beak will turn red if the bird is excited or angry.

Black Rhinoceros

A big, booming tank stomps down the hill. The black rhino is on its way to the watering hole.

This giant creature isn't really black. It is actually gray. Rhinos like to cool off by getting dirty. But the mud also makes them look darker. A nice mud bath makes the hot African sun easier to handle.

The dried mud on a rhino's skin also protects the animal from pesky flies.

Jewel Beetle

A shiny blue and gold shell shimmers in the sun. A jewel beetle sparkles on a flower.

This bright beetle looks pretty enough to wear, but don't be fooled. It uses the dazzling color as a disguise. Predators think this tasty creature is part of the plant.

Jewel beetles also use their bright colors to find mates.

Chameleon

Green skin turns yellow and then turns to red instead. The changing chameleon rests on a rock.

A chameleon's shade changes depending on its mood and temperature. It uses this clever color code to show how it feels. Color is one way chameleons communicate.

Many people think chameleons can change any color, but they can't. Their colors do include black, white, blue, green, red, and yellow.

Do You Remember?

Point to the picture of the animal described in each question.

1. The dried mud on my skin makes me look black.
   This baked-on color helps keep me cool. Who am I?

   (black rhinoceros)

2. My black and white colors help me hunt in the ocean.
   With this disguise, my prey can't see me. Who am I?

   (killer whale)

3. My bright green back looks just like a leaf. This color
   hides me during the day while I sleep. Who am I?

   (red-eyed treefrog)

Fun Facts

If a predator startles a red-eyed treefrog during the day, the frog's bright eyes pop open. The sudden red color usually scares the predator, giving the little treefrog time to escape.

The skin underneath a polar bear's fur is black. The dark color helps trap heat from the sun to keep the big animal warm in the cold Arctic.

Most rhinos, including the black rhinoceros and the white rhinoceros, are just different shades of gray.

Jewel beetles are so shiny and colorful that some people collect them. The bright bugs have been used in jewelry, art, and clothing.

Chameleons do not change color to match their surroundings. Their color changes according to their mood, temperature, and willingness to mate.

Glossary

communicate—trading or sharing thoughts, feelings, or other information

disguise—changing the way something looks in order to hide it or not show what it really is

horizontal—going across rather than up and down

mammals—animals that are warm-blooded and have a backbone

predator—an animal that hunts and eats other animals

prey—an animal that is hunted by another animal for food

vertical—up and down rather than across

TO LEARN MORE

At the Library

Arnosky, Jim. *I See Animals Hiding.* New York: Scholastic, 2000.

Otto, Carolyn B. *What Color Is Camouflage?* New York: HarperCollins, 1996.

Petty, Kate. *Animal Camouflage and Defense.* Philadelphia: Chelsea House, 2004.

On the Web

FactHound offers a safe, fun way to find Web sites related to this book.
All of the sites on FactHound have been researched by our staff.
www.facthound.com

1. Visit the FactHound home page.
2. Enter a search word related to this book, or type in this special code: 1404809317
3. Click the FETCH IT button.

Your trusty FactHound will fetch the best Web sites for you!

INDEX

Look for all of the books in the Animal Wise series:

Pointy, Long, or Round
A Book About Animal Shapes

Sand, Leaf, or Coral Reef
A Book About Animal Habitats

Stripes, Spots, or Diamonds
A Book About Animal Patterns

Red Eyes or Blue Feathers
A Book About Animal Colors

Strange Dances and Long Flights
A Book About Animal Behavior

Swing, Slither, or Swim
A Book About Animal Movements